CLOUDED CONTRAST

a collection of calamities

By: Steve Vanderweele

Clouded Contrast

Introduction

The drawings in this book
were scribbled by me
at a time when I was legally blind.
Advanced Diabetic Retinopathy
ravaged my life.
When I felt like I could
not express myself
I drew and wrote small blurbs
to release my feelings.
After years of sitting in
my desk I finally decided
to share them when I started
writing two years ago.
Within these pages live thoughts
and struggles with depression,
anxiety and the human psyche
dealing with a lifetime
of chronic illness.

Thank you.

Clouded Contrast

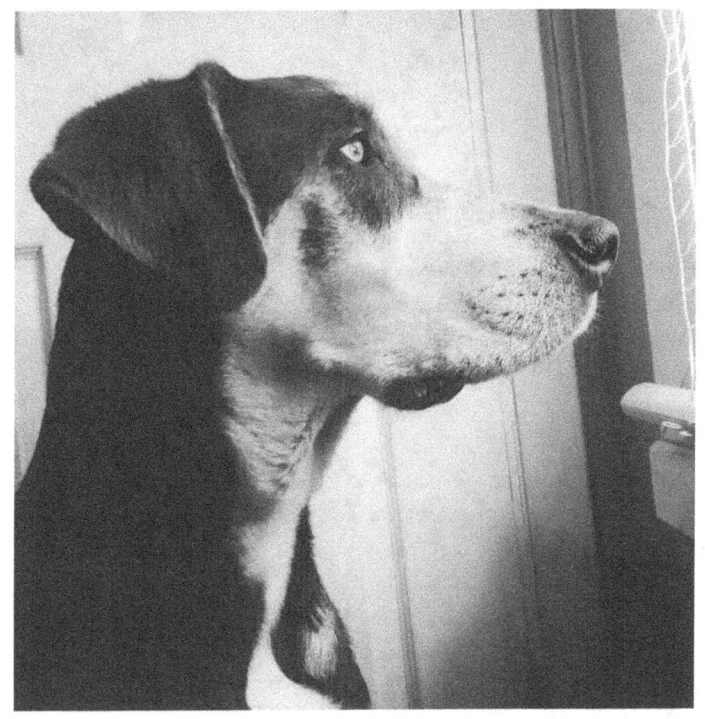

This book is dedicated
to my beautiful boy, Samson.
He passed away on July 3, 2024.

Clouded Contrast

Attempted Memories 5	No Heaven Alarms 42	March 2019 81
Pity Party 6	My Life 44	Daggers 82
Faded Heart 7	It's the Seed 45	Dead of Night 83
Star Counting 8	Medical Waste 46	Nice Heathen 84
Rotting Clock 9	Much More 47	Caution 86
S is for Steve 10	Chaos 49	Duality 88
A Needle or a Gun 12	K-Pin 50	Bitrate 89
Ask 13	Not 51	Cumbersome 90
Price of Humanity 14	Mmerika 52	Products 91
$ 15	Hollow 54	Humans 92
Toxins 16	Tight Rope 55	Downer 93
Annoyed 17	Proper Yield 57	Caught Up 95
Pictures 19	Lurking Night 58	Blind Observance 96
Slow Death 20	Taunting Whispers 59	Hidden 97
Dark Circles 21	Final Act 60	Family 98
6th Floor 22	Watershed 61	Time 99
Spotted Stones 23	Porous 62	Eye See You 100
Returning to Shore 24	Secrets 64	Barstool 102
From Below 27	Pile 65	Looped 103
Evaporated 28	Briar patch 67	Hungry for Life 105
Modern Dirt 29	Friend Unwanted 68	DKA 106
Flooded 30	Dig Deep 69	Opposite 107
Inside Storms 31	Remain 70	Harmonious 109
Release 32	Curb Appeal 72	Anxiety Surprise 111
Parts Lost 34	No hue 73	Night and Day 112
Ghostly Words 35	In-between 74	Thoughts I Fight 113
Lost or Gone 36	Perception 76	Comfort Zone 114
Midnight Lows 37	Look Closely 77	Four Walls 115
Problem Child 39	Waltz 78	If Only 117
Haunted 40	Listen 80	Battle Scars 118

Clouded Contrast

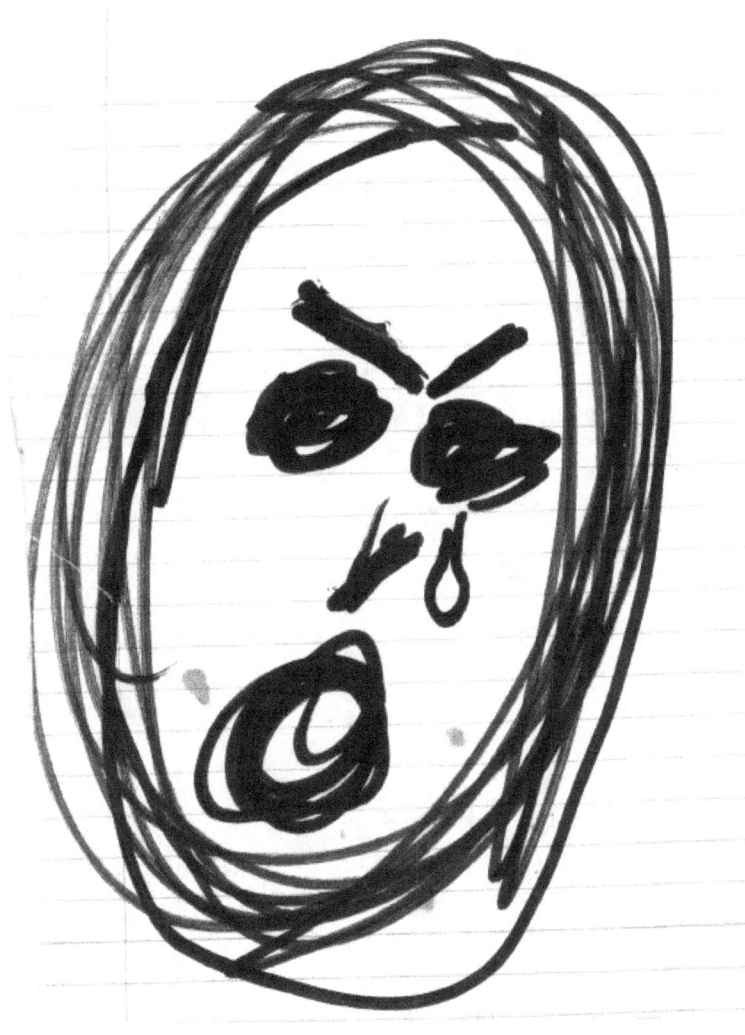

Clouded Contrast

Attempted Memories

I can barely remember a time

that part of me

didn't want to die.

It's always been lurking,

consistently working

to commandeer the throne.

There once was a bloodless coup

when I chose to no longer try.

I've always done better on my own,

but damn,

on that day I've never felt so alone.

Clouded Contrast

Pity Party

I've got some nerve damage
and a couple of diseases,
but don't feel sorry for me.
Because my jokes about it
will crash the pity party
like a kite without a breeze.
So, smile at the dark comedy
that is my life and be happy
that I'm still breathing.

Clouded Contrast

Faded Heart

I wear a faded black hat
with a heart to match.
I get too attached
or take three steps back.
There's not much intact,
so I'll continue to crack.
I'm on a mad dash to find a path.
But I'll come in last
because I'm running from my past.

Clouded Contrast

Star Counting

I followed the moon
and ended up at the shore
to count the stars.
To look out at the shifting tide
while burying all my scars.
To put them deep in the sands of time,
Covered; so they can't be found.
Down in the deafening dark,
so they'd never make another sound.
But as the sunlight wakes the day,
all of my battles rise again.
And as they crawl to the surface,
waters come rushing in.

Clouded Contrast

Rotting Clock

I let myself rot

while staring at the clock.

But I forgot

I was crafting a lock.

A lock to box

for my thoughts

that knock.

Knocking around my head

like a bucket of rocks.

So I'll stop looking

at every tick

and every tock.

And not be blocked

by the thought

of my burial plot.

Clouded Contrast

S is for Steve

A sarcastically surviving

but stoic soul

shouts in solitude,

singing songs

of suffering and sorrow

while silently soaring

through scarlet skies.

Clouded Contrast

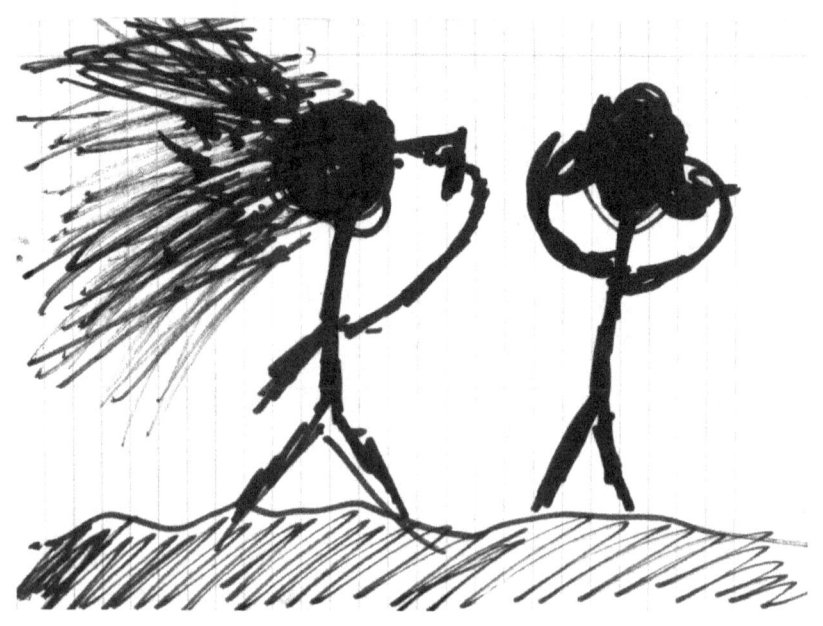

Clouded Contrast

A Needle or a Gun

I held a syringe to my arm
like a gun to my head.
I knew it'd work
if I killed my instincts first.
All I wanted was to leave the page
by writing my own end.
I pushed the plunger in
and hoped for the worst.
Like pulling the trigger,
and expecting death.
Yet we're programmed to live,
even if cursed.

Clouded Contrast

Ask

Go ahead,

peel me back and ask.

I'll spill it all

with my hands neatly folded

on my lap.

I'll tell you what I am,

who I was, and what I lack.

But if it's used to attack

I'll ask you to get the fuck back.

Clouded Contrast

Price of Humanity

Bright starry nights
faded into ominously tinted skies.
A rushing river depleted
down to pale scars on the earth.
Lakes, oceans and seas
infected by billions of absent minds.
Luscious woodlands split and cut,
making room for new capital growth.
The natural world
sold off to the quickest bidder
for the greatest price.
A bill we cannot pay,
destroying our only worth.

Clouded Contrast

$

Money money money.
How's it make you feel?
Fuck the goddamn number.
Give me something real.
Honesty is honestly
all I really need.
So I'll keep it level with you
if you keep it straight with me.

Clouded Contrast

Toxins

We are all

being poisoned

by something.

Whether it's

imagined or real.

The trick is

to recognize

the toxin

before the cure.

Clouded Contrast

Annoyed

Fuck a filter and the
toxic beauty standards.
Forget the cookie cutter trends
of copy and paste "influencers".
Don't look through their lens
or abide by their rules.
I'm sick of the fake and vapid mules.
Smuggling a skewed interoperation
of worth that corrupts the soul.
They peddle it and spread it
like their lives depend on the sale.
I don't fit into this
showboating world.
But that's fine with me,
because I only mingle with people
who question what's being sold.

Clouded Contrast

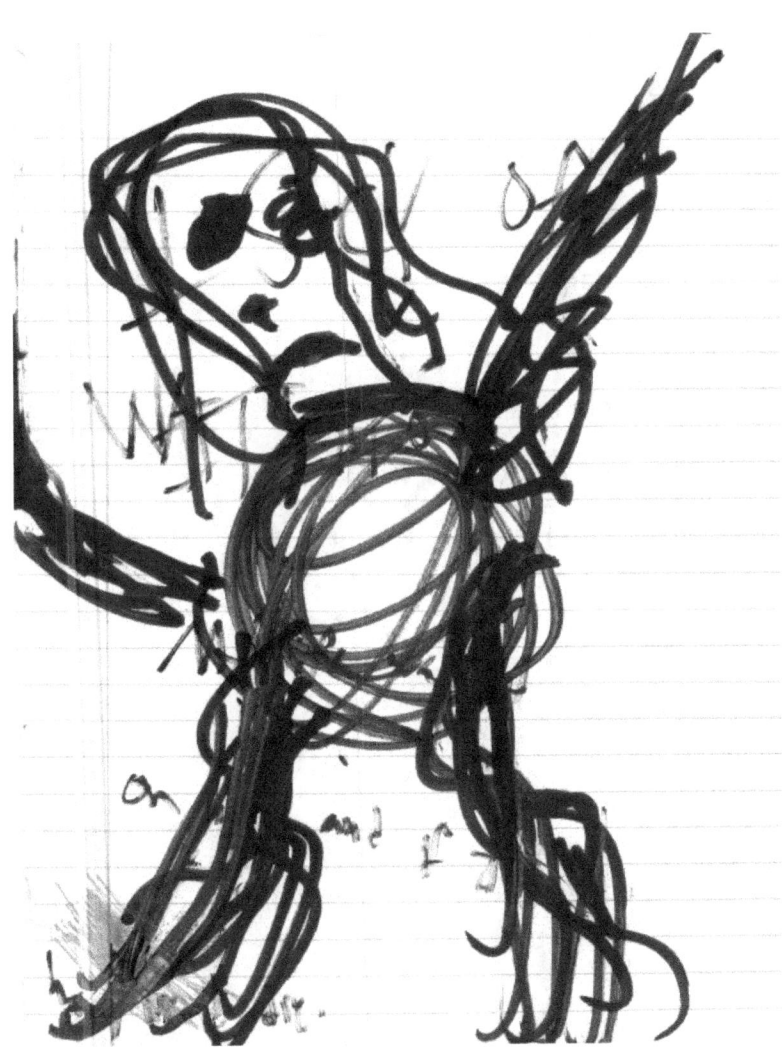

Clouded Contrast

Pictures

If a picture

is worth

a thousand words,

I wonder

how many images

it would take

to represent

the sentences

that endlessly disturb.

Clouded Contrast

Slow Death

I am bleeding out slow,
I don't know why it won't clot.
Wounded from years ago,
so far back that I forgot.
It plays with my ego,
reminding me the knife is hot
and cuts down to the bone.
It tells me what I'm not
and churns deep within my soul.

Clouded Contrast

Dark Circles

> I wear dark clothes
> from a dark wardrobe
> that match the circles
> around my eyes.
> They let others know
> that I don't sleep alone,
> but with the shadows
> of my mind.

Clouded Contrast

6th Floor

Cold floors,

hands and toes.

A sterile room,

bed and clothes.

Beeping

droning

and knocking.

Aching,

waking

and poking.

White walls,

gloves and coats.

Empty chairs,

cups and hopes.

Lonesome,

sickly and scared.

Skinny and weak,

barely even there.

Clouded Contrast

Spotted Stones

I hold no expectations.

I'll walk on the edge

and pocket hope

like spotted stones

buried on the shore.

It's a defense mechanism.

My pockets are full of holes,

so when I reach the water

I'll sink no more.

Clouded Contrast

Returning to Shore

I want to fall for my own con.
To believe that I can
work out the knots.
To see the horizon
as vividly obtainable,
rather than a dim and cloudy
fog of denial.
I want to fool myself with hope,
rather than knowing that
it's all just a show.
Words are curiously
keeping me afloat.
Actions accidentally
poke holes in the boat.
Thoughts push me further
from the coast.

Clouded Contrast

As I drift,

the cold truth

begins to unfold.

It's broad and heavy,

but still curable.

I can mend it though,

even with the obstacles.

Then I'll hoist it high

and tie it taut.

To let the wind take me where I belong.

Clouded Contrast

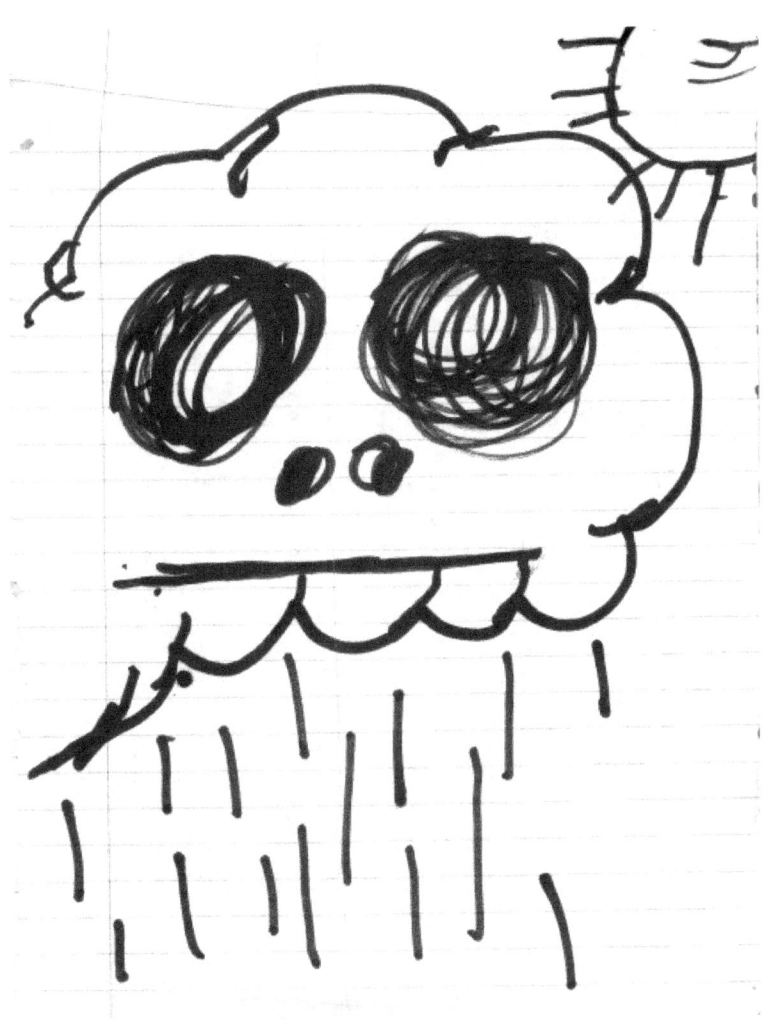

Clouded Contrast

From Below

The clouds came crashing down
with malevolent force.
Violent waves witnessed
from the grit of the seafloor.
Pushed here and there,
breathless in beautiful turbulence.
The weight of the world
shattered a calm blue surface.
Breaking the plane of existence
without questioning the crowd.
Swirling and pulling the sediment
in the bubbling waters of doubt.

Clouded Contrast

Evaporated

I am like vapor,

seen but never held,

immersed but never felt.

Lingering on the skin,

but never seeping in.

Condensed to evaporate,

It's there but it is known

to disappear.

Clouded Contrast

Modern Dirt

Kill the sky.

Burn the land

and poison the ocean.

Create the cloud.

Buy the dirt

and dam the river.

Trade the blame.

Sell the lie

and hide the graves.

Clouded Contrast

Flooded

Clouds of hard truth
are moving in again.
Pouring thoughts
feel like a severed brainstem.
Puddles of forgotten barbs
start to form.
While long-lost hopes and failures
maintain the storm.

        The levies broke and soon
        these lowlands will flood.
        So, there is nowhere to go,
                nowhere but up.

Clouded Contrast

Inside Storms

There's a storm coming.
It's a late summer
thundering downpour.
It turns shimmering midday
into a drab sun setting.
Crying as it roars.
Pounding from above,
lashing out with
overwhelmed aggression.
Flowing in the streets and
warping the way home;
shaking with tension.
It howls and pushes,
cracking unstable
foundations with ease.
Trapping all in a cold
and noisy darkness.
Destroying the peace.

Clouded Contrast

Release

Go stand out in the rain
on one of those sticky summer days.
Let the rat race wash off like dust
and sink your toes into the mud.
Feel the pressure quickly fall around
you and release it all.
If only for a second,
try to feel like a kid again.

Clouded Contrast

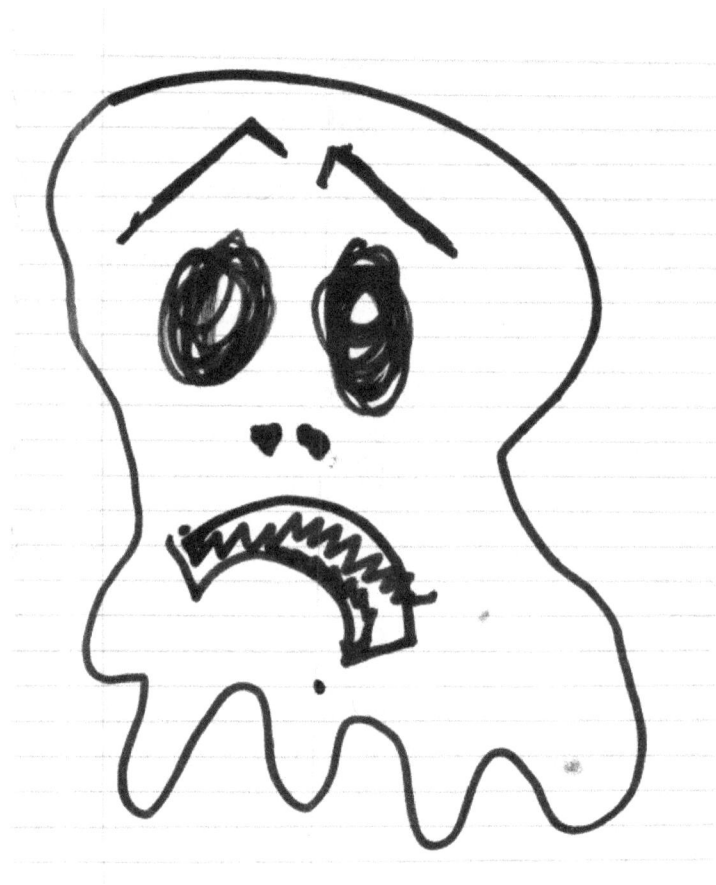

Clouded Contrast

Parts Lost

I wanted all of me to be gone
with my fatal attempt.
But only part of me faded away
to ash, back to dirt.
I don't know where to look,
or what to call out to make it return.
How to see myself in this place
and walk around as I once did.
Not pretend, but live,
forget this nonsense that is
pointless but ruthless.

Clouded Contrast

Ghostly Words

Cold words rest on the back of my neck.
The hair stands at attention.
They live only in a ghostly breath.
Ghouls in a shroud of perception.
Sliding up my spine, reaching my mind.
Spreading out and hunkering down.
Growing in strength as they multiply.
Crowding the stages all over town.
Destroying logic by casting lies.

Clouded Contrast

Lost or Gone?

I
cannot
find
me,
I
hope
I
am
only
lost,
and
not
gone
completely.

Clouded Contrast

Midnight Lows

False realities are projected,
consisting of familiar people
in a nonsensical loop.
Twenty feet feels like
a thousand miles
through a thick and hazy soup.
Blinking tremors,
twitching fingers,
a warning with repetition
of sudden falling.
A hollow feeling,
completely empty.
Sweat runs from every pore,
soaking through the sheets
making everything droop.

Clouded Contrast

Sometimes music can be heard,

an upbeat hallucination

in the silence,

backed up by my

heart pounding.

It's a tragic melody,

conducted by a dying symphony

luring me to the abyss of no recoup.

Clouded Contrast

Problem Child

A disheveled mess,

homegrown,

planted in the nest.

No one is to blame,

the fractured mirror

is reflecting only shame.

Always late,

content with last place.

Clouded Contrast

Haunted

I'll draw you in with words
and a loathing for the herd
that inhabits this earth.
You'll stay for a while to wait and see
if the worn down
will one day come clean.
To see if all these thoughts
could be taught to stop
and one day be caught.
But they will not leave,
nor listen to me,
they only corrupt and spread the disease.
So don't get too close,
I'm the man without hope,
a living, but incurable ghost.

Clouded Contrast

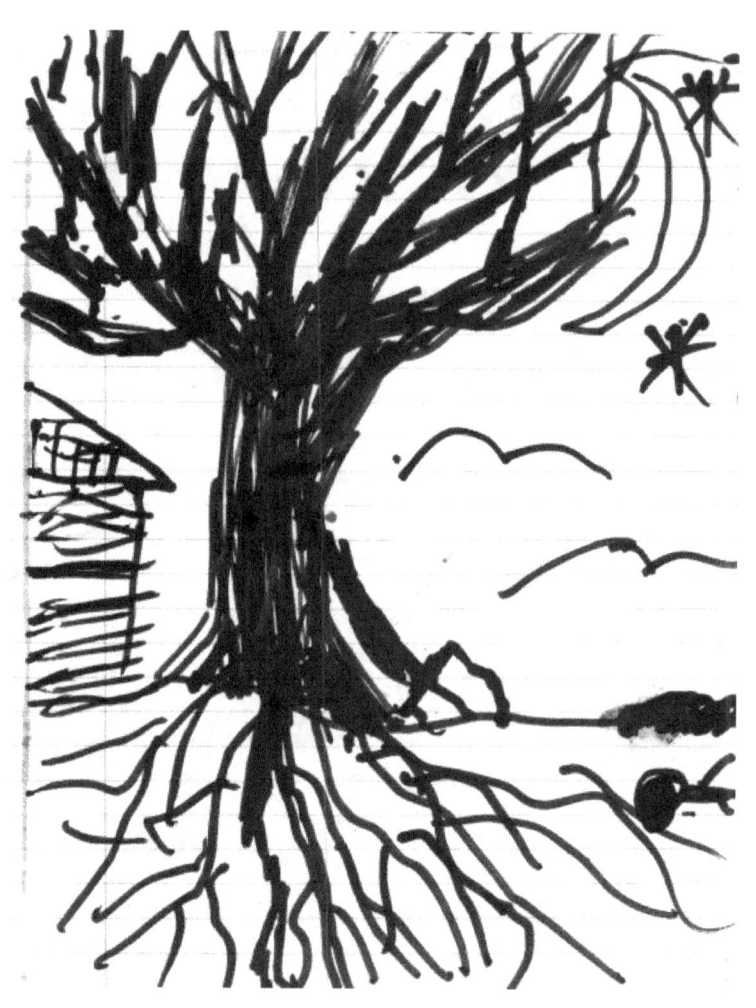

Clouded Contrast

No Heaven Alarms

I have no savior, no gods,
no all-powerful keeping
a tally of my behavior.
No prayers to send,
no devil tempting my fate
and no heaven alarms on weekends.
No conflicting stories,
or chosen path to a gilded gate
and no hand-me-down fallacies.
No salvation bought,
no pamphlet of control,
no punishment for thought.
I have logic with reasoning,
free thinking guided by researching
and a chronic illness
that shaped my awareness.
I've got decades of struggle with a few
overactive and usually nervous muscles.

Clouded Contrast

I have lessons branded on my mind,

bits of scattered knowledge

and always one eye on the time.

I've got a soft heart

that melts easily,

but I cover it up with dead branches

and piles of jagged opportunities.

Clouded Contrast

My Life

I am the architect and the janitor,
the dirt and the gardener.

Clouded Contrast

It's the Seed

I have tried to settle into a life,
remove my walking shoes and grow roots.
Right here, over there,
with them, with her,
in this, in that and the other.
So that leads me to believe
that one of them is toxic,
either the soil or the seed.
And based on the rate of success,
it looks like the poison
resides within me.

Clouded Contrast

Medical Waste

What if you don't deserve me,
and that's not what you think it means.
You do not deserve the pain I will
cause with the nights I'll take, or to
be caught in my self-destructive wake.
You do not deserve the many parking lot
and love validations that comes with
notching hospital visitations.
You do not deserve to struggle in
uncertainty, because the system
feeds on the weak and the broken.
You do not deserve to watch the
one you love lose hope
along with appendages
or to be alone at family functions.
A partner slowly decaying
from circumstance isn't a
viable option in this world,
lingering on a chance.

Clouded Contrast

Much More

ADHD and a bit neurotic.
I am what I am,
but I am much more
of what I am not.
I can't not be me,
anything else
makes me rot.

Clouded Contrast

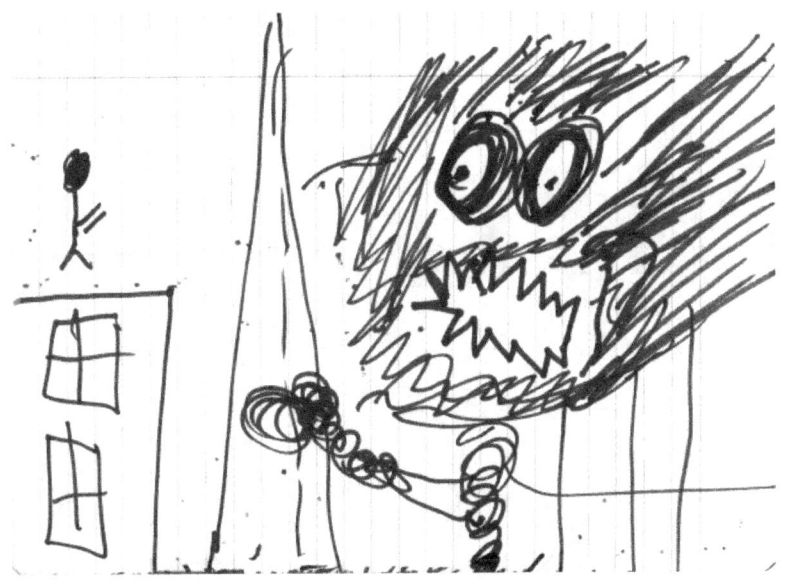

Clouded Contrast

Chaos

I am

a disaster happening,

waiting to unfold,

and the aftermath

all at once.

Clouded Contrast

K-Pin

The pills are nails
and these four walls my coffin.
Dissolving all detail
as the drown my perception.
Killing every thought
while growing the habit.
Nothing more is sought
if I still have them.
Prescribed to get through,
but they only got me stuck.
I feel nothing new
and I no longer look up.

Clouded Contrast

Not

not a sheep

not a wolf

something

in-between

Clouded Contrast

Mmerika

We're being killed
with pleasant distractions
and formulated addictive conveniences.
Slowly strangled to death
with carefully spun manipulations
of what happiness is.
We run each other over for trophies
and trinkets of legacy in a race
that is stomping us out.
Because we're worn thin
from staying in line
so we can bleed to put food
in our mouths.
A choice between
treading water or drowning while
shooting signal flares.
Under a lens of spewed memorization
that records no depth,
just the what, the when, and the where.

Clouded Contrast

We are a bunch of want-to-be

trendy whores conditioned to

forget the clandestine

filth of society.

But we are forced to live

on hope alone,

which only grows

the malignant tumors

that are exponentially

killing humanity.

Clouded Contrast

Hollow

With eyes filling,

flustered breath

and formidable thinking,

I drag myself up

from the deadening.

I crawl away from

the frigidly numb

and drastically hollow feeling

that follows me endlessly.

… Clouded Contrast

Tight Rope

One self-loving step at a time,
I try to balance on the line
between what's left and what has died.
But it's pulled tight
and strung-up high,
dividing the light in the sky
from the dark mistakes of my life.
And if there is slack in the line
it seems to suddenly remind
that I could fall at any time.
However, I'll still stride
across the gaps in my mind
because I can finally
see the other side.

Clouded Contrast

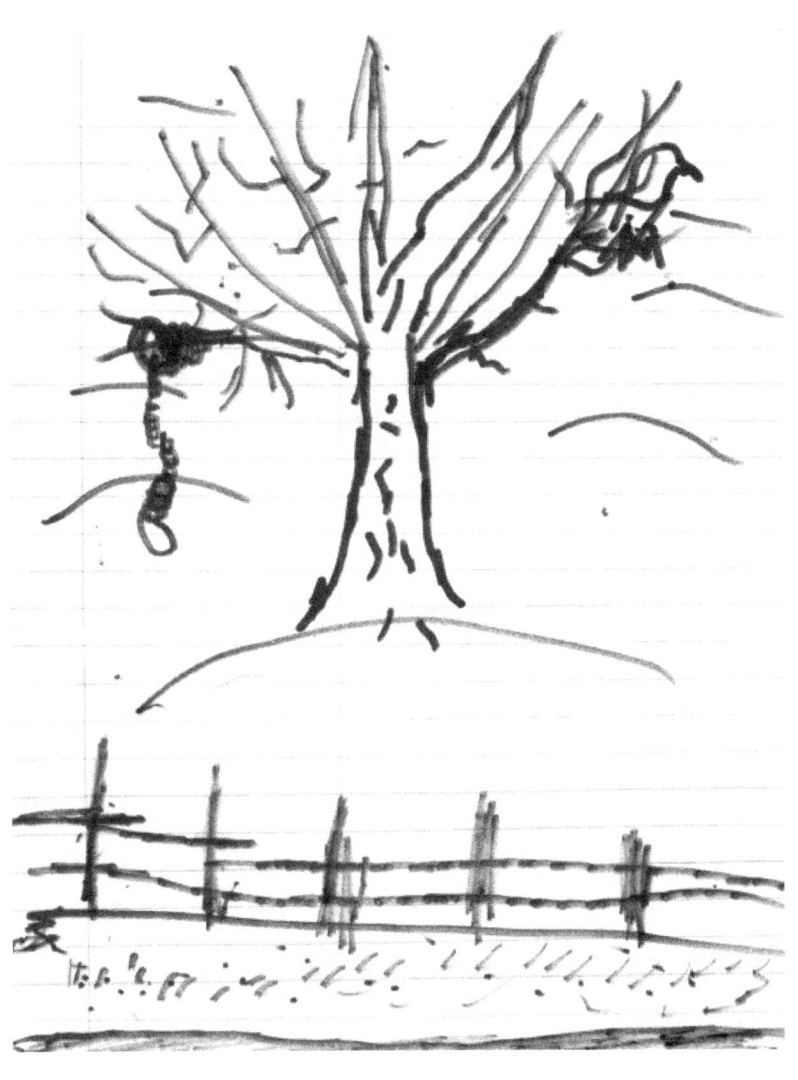

Clouded Contrast

Proper Yield

Like a garden

planted in the forest,

you need to space your efforts

according to the trees.

Otherwise,

you'll have no yield

from

the

crops

beneath.

Clouded Contrast

Lurking Night

It's hard to find light
as death lurches from the dark.
While it's easy to hide in the night
if you never make your mark.

Clouded Contrast

Taunting Whispers

A rope braided from lost hope
hangs in the wind.
It taunts while it swings
with the haunting breeze.
Laughing hard
at a past life creeping in.
It's waiting and knocking
against the tree.
Tempting thoughts that make
the shaking begin.
It's trapping time
with knotted memories,
causing it to scrape away
at paper thin skin.
And it whispers desires
to let me finally be free.

Clouded Contrast

Final Act

I
mistook
intermission
for
the
end of my play.
And
now
I
am
locked
in
the
lobby
lying in wait.

Clouded Contrast

Watershed

A quiet stream
connects
with a
chaotic river
spiraling
downward.
It's
desperately
searching
the vast
and wild watershed.
Continuously
reaching out
for a
peaceful lake
in which to empty.

Clouded Contrast

Porous

Carved out by the rain
and set there by the
weight of creation,
a single lone boulder
on the plains of stagnation is waiting.
It's stuck in the earth,
substantial but full of holes
stippled by timeless glaciers.
It is heavy by design,
dense and yet porous
from dust colliding with the surface.
Hoping for the ground to shift,
to release its destructive hold.
It has been here too long
and has stories
about being alone.

Clouded Contrast

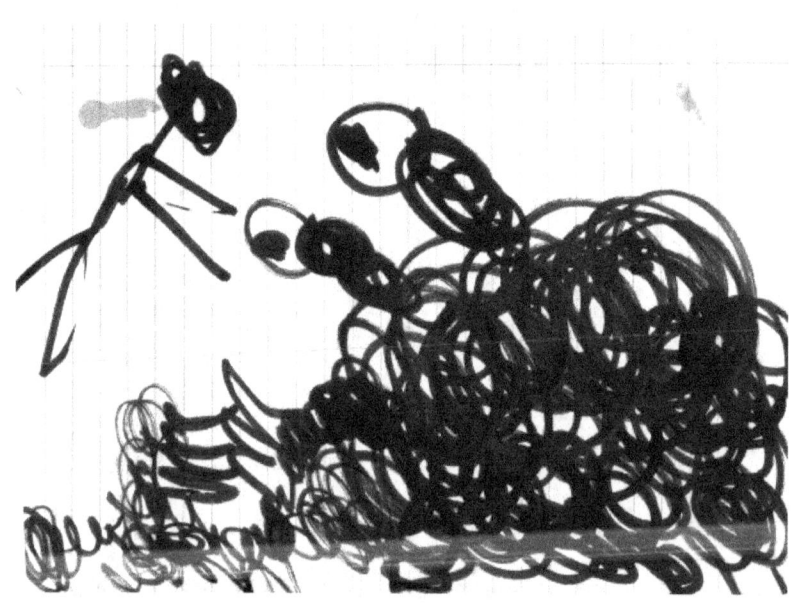

Clouded Contrast

Secrets

Sleeping soundly

on a layer of ash.

Comfortably surrounded

by stacks of trash.

Listening closely to the words,

only seeing motion blurs.

Stumbling again back to bed

while mumbling secrets to the dead.

Clouded Contrast

Pile

"Smile like you mean it."
What an ignorant thing to say.
Trained to be complacent,
quiet and out of the way.

"Put a smile on your face."
What a simple suggestion.
Can't look to be out of place.
If you do, you'll be questioned.

"You should smile more."
What a mindless sentence.
Thinking it'll open the door,
but it's gone from existence.

Clouded Contrast

Don't tell me to smile.

I laugh, play and grin a lot.

But some days I'm a pile,

beneath a heap of thought.

Clouded Contrast

Briar Patch

Lines crossed
but not a single i dotted.
A trail in my mind
that leads to something rotten.
A tree of self-tapped toxins
are jarred and quickly sold.
It's bad business,
but I get sick of the cold.
A house of mirrors,
but I can't stand the view.
It's cracked and faded,
but the glass is brand new.
A briar-patch is where
I lay my head at night.
It cuts as it grows
and slowly squeezes me tight.

Clouded Contrast

Friend Unwanted

It leaks out of my soul
with a vengeful fury.
And I shake my head,
disagreeing with the feeling.
Sometimes it stays for days,
reclaiming its fame.
And sometimes
it flies straight away,
like a moth chasing a flame.

Clouded Contrast

Dig Deep

Let us dance within the human psyche,
and fall deep until we decipher happy.
We'll become entangled by
the waves inside;
embrace the strange and enjoy the ride.
We'll find the truth to what
stubbornly rests
beneath the chest and above the neck.
Let's not waste all our dreams
while sleeping.
But hold them close
on the days we feel like screaming.

Clouded Contrast

Remain

Do not fret

my downtrodden friends.

I know it's dark,

but you'll find peace

before the end.

Stay true

and remain persistent

through the sludge

of this world's

resistance.

Clouded Contrast

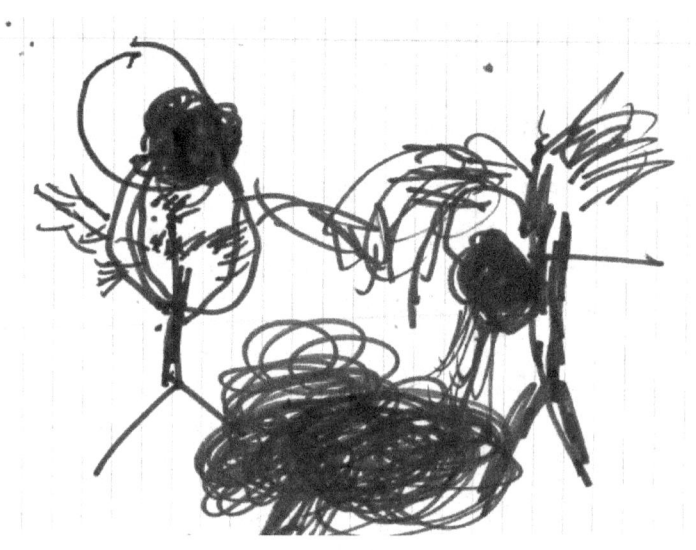

Clouded Contrast

Curb Appeal

The

need

to

achieve

perfection

by

making

it

all

nice

and

neat,

new

and

immaculately

clean

will one day kill you and me.

Clouded Contrast

No Hue

You don't want me,
even if you think you do.
So don't say please.
I am a man with no hue,
I am riddled with disease.
A storm just passing through,
a shell of a body,
destructively empty.
So even if you think you do,
trust me, you don't want me.
And you especially don't
want me, wanting you.

Clouded Contrast

In-between

I'm stuck somewhere between
life and death.
I find myself not wanting either.
So what do I do, where do I go?
Don't answer, that was rhetorical.
I've been depressed,
but this feels like something else.
I've been anxious,
but this is something else.
It's not me, but it is.
It's uncomfortable I know.
But I have nothing left.
I am just being honest.
People ignore the truth nowadays.
I'm not a person, I am merely a haze.
A blur of a man without purpose.
Without meaning or reason.
So why prolong the burden I am.

Clouded Contrast

I want to say goodbye,

but I can't find the words.

I want to leave town,

but I can't see the road.

Clouded Contrast

Perception

Delightful lies

cultivate delusional truth.

Undignified words

decay the roots.

Degrading actions

stick like superglue.

Deny the sky,

but only when it's blue.

Clouded Contrast

Look Closely

Barriers and walls,

locks and gates

to ward off the curious.

A savagely sudden silence

to prove that I'm serious.

The unlucky ones will perceive it

as something mysterious.

But the allure ends there my dear.

So don't misconstrue the precarious

for anything that could be glorious.

Clouded Contrast

Waltz

I move in three quarter time,
swaying back and forth
to keep myself alive.
That signature is a friend.
A good old pal that dances
when I walk in.
I'm connected to the bassline.
A shared past of downbeats
and sad story rhymes.
It will be there in the end.
When the others
are too busy to attend.

Clouded Contrast

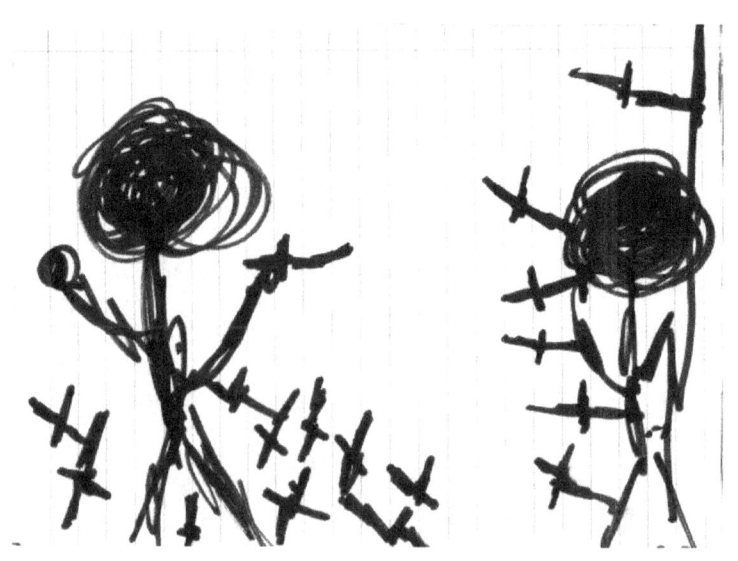

Clouded Contrast

Listen

You

should

listen

to

the

angel

on

my

shoulder,

for

it

warns

of

the

devil

on

the

other.

Clouded Contrast

March 2019

I killed my spirit on that lonely day
in the cold of early March.
I was trying to end my saga
before it ever had a hope to start.
I gathered a funeral parade
and struck my own bell.
There were no flames
or brimstone pits,
but still I awoke in hell.
I guess you could say,
that I got more
than I bargained for.
I was expecting nothing,
but I got my troubles back,
with even more than before.

Clouded Contrast

Daggers

I was melted down

and now I'm pouring out.

I was hammered

with narcissistic words

as daggers emerged.

And quenched in waters form,

so please ignore the warp.

Clouded Contrast

Dead of Night

My scars become knives
in the dead of night,
cutting me up as I wipe away
the tears from a past life.
Memories of what I'd be
and what I used to see
grow dense clouds of doubt
that are killing me.
Slowly slashing and tearing
my worn-out soul to bits.
Causing a monotonous death
by a thousand cuts and pricks.

Clouded Contrast

Nice Heathen

I am nice,

like the point of an ice-cold knife

held to the wrist each night.

I am neat,

like a cheap whiskey

that sinks in deep,

revealing that feeling of defeat.

I am funny,

like a tragically bad ending

to a muddy story

in made for T.V. movie.

I am crude,

like telling the truth

about how ruthlessly

this world deludes.

Clouded Contrast

I am a lot,

like how my thoughts

respond rather than stop

at end of the knot.

I am a heathen,

because to me Jesus

was just a man

who may have known some

sleight of hand.

Clouded Contrast

Caution

Be careful if you cut corners
because you might run into a wall.
Be cautious while walking on the edge
because you might fall.

Clouded Contrast

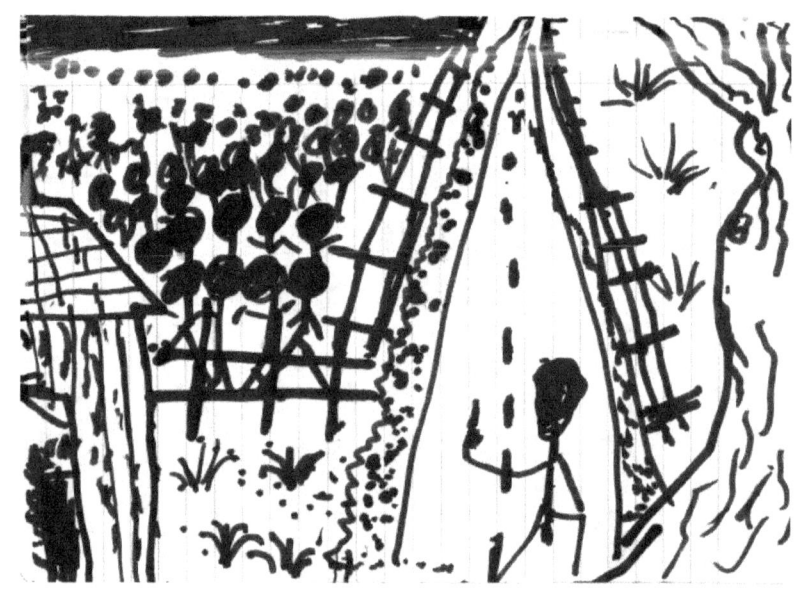

Clouded Contrast

Duality

Some days I feel like
just another scumbag
wasting away
on this ball of dirt.

                    And some days I think I'm
                            one of a kind,
                        breathing in time
                  and exhaling the earth.

Clouded Contrast

Bitrate

I'm stuck buffering in the
streaming service of this world.
Bandwidth at an all-time low
from neighborhoods about to burst.
Everyone's looking to binge
and then move on with the current.
Trendy entertainment at our fingertips,
we are nothing more than servants.

Clouded Contrast

Cumbersome

I don't like the world
so I tried to build my own.
But the weight of my design
has grown cumbersome.
I am no Atlas,
so I am letting go
and watching it burn.
I'm more like Atlantis,
sunken deep in the waves that turn.
Somewhere in-between legend
and a mythical power unknown.
But truly I am just
another part of existence,
with scraps to be resown.

Clouded Contrast

Products

I am not meant to be here,

I just happen to be.

A mere product of

circumstance and biology.

We're not supposed to go this way,

it's just the most convenient.

Following strung up dreams

and then selling them to pay rent.

Clouded Contrast

Humans

An infestation killing over
ancestral rights to invade and pray.
Complaining while taking
and smiling while the host decays.
Spreading and suffocating
without a sliver of shame.
A greedy parasite,
that refuses to accept the blame.

Clouded Contrast

Downer

I'm

not

a

downer,

reality

knocked

me

flat,

truth

can

be

humbling.

Clouded Contrast

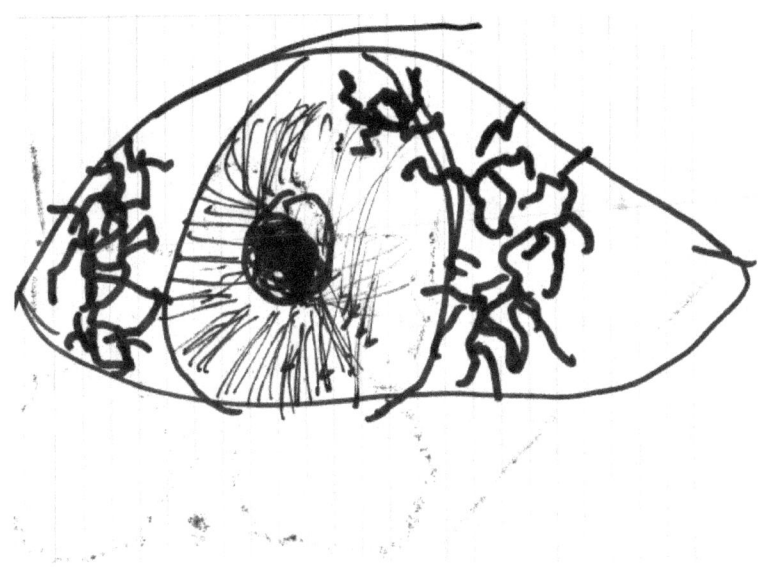

Clouded Contrast

Caught up

Tomorrow's a bet,

a childish game of chance

that favors the net.

Clouded Contrast

Blind Observance

There's someone at the door.
I know because
I felt them walk up on the porch.
New things are discovered.
Like hot and cold water
sound different when poured.
I'm forced to move slowly.
So now I take every single gait safely.
I'm tired of tripping.
Sick of counting the steps between
to avoid pity.
I'm lost out in space.
And it has been weeks
since I last saw a face.
I miss seeing the day.
I'm stuck in my head,
chained in bed,
staring at shapes.

Clouded Contrast

Hidden

These hard times
are foolishly of my own
negligent design.
Remembering my way
through this self-destructive path
that I've lined.
The silent lies run around,
keeping me up late into the night.
Waiting for the light
reminds me that I kept it
hidden out of sight.
Falling asleep just in time
to miss the sunrise.
Waking up surprised
and forgetting that I am still alive.

Clouded Contrast

Family

My hands are calloused like my father's
and my heart is soft like my mother's.
I am creative because of my sister
and I am intelligent because
of my brothers.

Clouded Contrast

Time

You cannot hold it in your hands,
though you can feel it in your bones.
It cannot be planted or harvested,
but it is always being consumed.
You can lose it easily
but rarely is it found.
It can be given, taken and killed,
passed, remembered and forgotten,
wasted, lost and filled.
It is a continuously
consistent constant.
It is held so close and cherished,
but can feel so distant.

Clouded Contrast

Eye See You

A faded sparkle,

kind eyes live in broken hearts,

they see through the dark.

Clouded Contrast

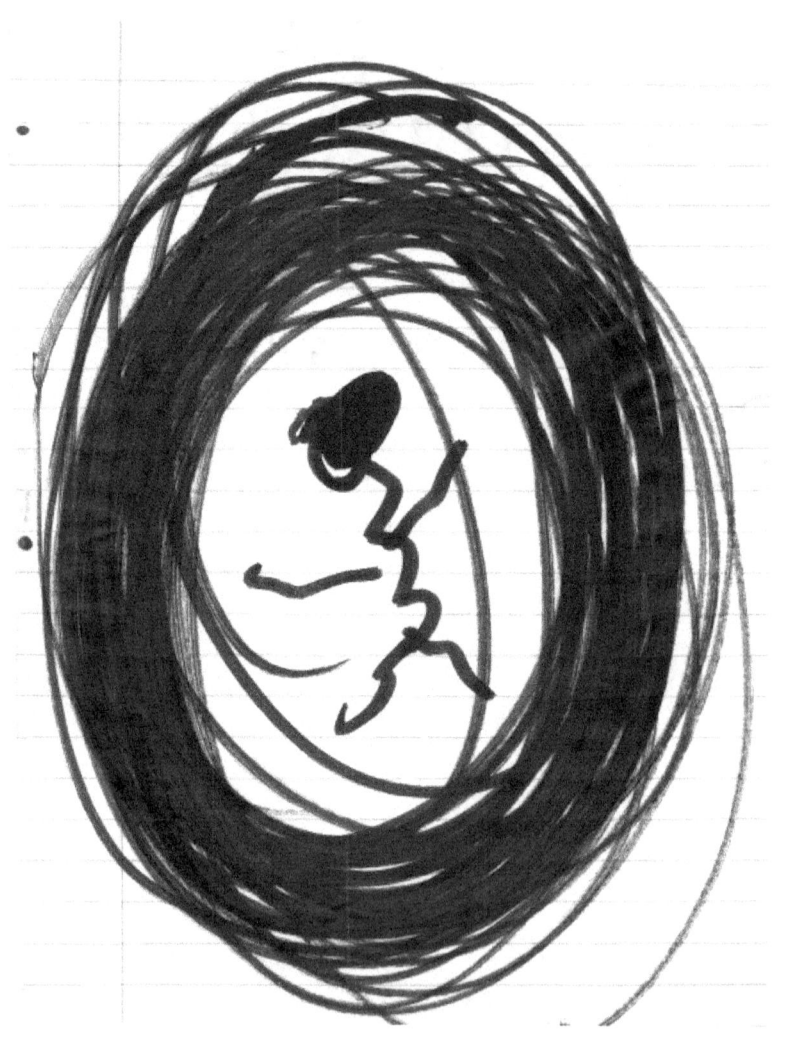

Clouded Contrast

Barstool

I am a barstool,

unused

atop a dimly lit stage

on open mic night.

Clouded Contrast

Looped

I stay too long in the
underworld of my mind,
wading through the thick pools
of muddy thoughts.
People I knew, what they said,
that look in their eyes,
and what they did.
The person I am, the way I react,
what is perception, and what is fact.
Nothing is permanent,
it's just an illusion,
the world is dying,
all the unneeded confusion.
Value misplaced, the world is dying,
we just want distractions,
and the world is dying.

Clouded Contrast

The universal hologram,

the world is dying,

and we're killing the soul

along with ourselves.

Clouded Contrast

Hungry for Life

Starved

by

the

present,

dragged back

and forth

by the past;

my future

is

dormant.

Clouded Contrast

DKA

It hurts to move,

but that's nothing new.

So here I lay,

wide awake.

The knife in my gut

turns while it cuts.

My skin is sunken

and my breath is stubborn.

I'm on the floor again,

needing intravenous hydration.

I am past my limit,

guess it's time for

another hospital visit.

Clouded Contrast

Opposite

Happiness rarely

comprehends sadness.

And when it does,

it usually comes from death.

But that's more of a duality

rather than an understanding.

And it's usually the greed

of joy that brings sorrow.

For how could the sky relate

to the molten core of the earth?

And how could the water

know what it is to be dirt?

The key is for both

to accept the other

without stipulation.

No promises for

one to become better

Clouded Contrast

should be required.

And all too often sadness

is the one extending

the olive branch

to its counterpart.

Clouded Contrast

Harmonious

Every

    one

        of

            us

        is

    tilted

and

    spinning.

Clouded Contrast

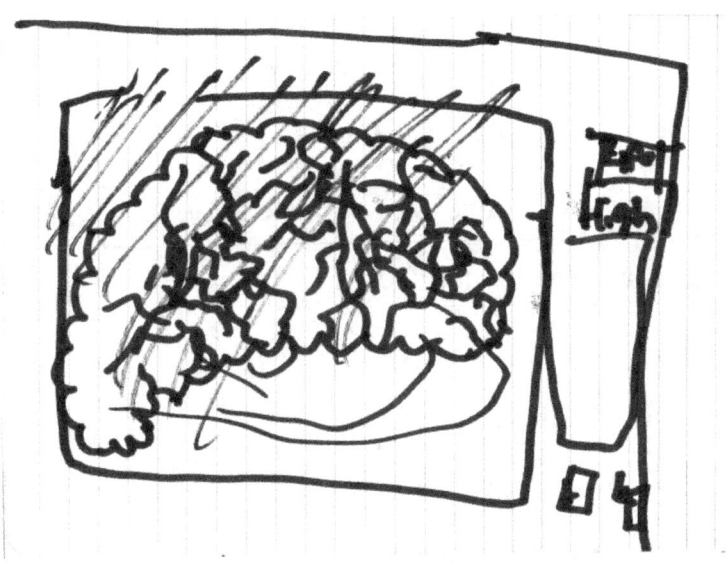

Clouded Contrast

Anxiety Surprise

Pragmatic possibilities,
        provoking perfectly.
Sarcastic stupidities,
        swirling secretly.
Engrossing eventualities,
        evolving endlessly.
Rigid redundancies,
        raging relentlessly.
Formidable fantasies,
        fighting frantically.
Caustic commonalities,
        creeping cautiously.

Clouded Contrast

Night and Day

My

nights

are

spent

imagining

calamities.

My

days

are

filled

with

tragically

familiar

realities.

Clouded Contrast

Thoughts I Fight

It's too late

to mount a defense,

too expensive.

I'm too pathetic,

too depressive.

Neurotic.

Regressive.

I'm not worth it,

just another person,

nothing special.

Change the station.

Turn the dial.

Leave me on the pavement.

Sink me in the ocean.

Clouded Contrast

Comfort Zone

A comfort zone becomes a prison.
The walls are built
taller by indecision.
Bars thicken while
it's bright on the other side.
Held in a shrinking cell,
burning away time.
The guards do everything I say.
Everything except let me escape.

Clouded Contrast

Four Walls

Four walls with two doors,

I can't see it

but I can hear the downpour.

Today is yesterday

and tomorrow will be the same but more.

Four walls inside of four walls

with two doors sealed up.

It could be half full or half empty,

either way, it's poison in my cup.

Two doors housing four locks

with the walls watching

and taking stock.

Lots of thoughts and

listened to fiction kill the clock.

Clouded Contrast

Four walls inside four walls

with two doors

holding four locks

with one key.

Restricted and waiting,

contemplating the day of retreat.

Clouded Contrast

If Only

    If we could only realize

    that all of us are the gods,

    and that the natural world

    is our holy kingdom,

    we might all be better off.

    If we listen to the earth

    like followers of religion,

    we could be the first

    to hear the prayers...

    and actually be able

    to answer them.

Clouded Contrast

Battle Scars

Some battles

draw scars.

Those marks

are a blueprint

to build

the ramparts

and burn

the drawbridge.

www.ingramcontent.com/pod-product-compliance
Lightning Source LLC
Chambersburg PA
CBHW071036240526
45469CB00006BD/2223